Contents

KV-374-275

⚽⚽⚽⚽⚽⚽⚽⚽⚽⚽⚽⚽⚽⚽⚽⚽⚽⚽⚽⚽⚽

PERSONAL PROFILE

5

Quick quote

A true fan is one who supports his or her team come what may, through thick or thin, promotion or relegation, ups and downs, ins or outs, no matter what it costs.

Personal info

@@@@@@@@@@@@@@@@@@@@

....

Name
....

Nickname
....

Address
....

....

Telephone
....

Mobile phone
....

Email
....

Date of birth
....

Height
....

Weight
....

Boot size
....

Shirt size
....

Old football boots
(probably worn
to play against
the Romans!)

7

Football school

⚽⚽⚽⚽⚽⚽⚽⚽⚽⚽⚽⚽⚽⚽⚽⚽⚽⚽⚽⚽⚽

Team name

Team nickname

Team strip

Position I like playing best

Position I usually play

Number of matches played

Number of goals scored

Most brilliant match ever

Worst foul on me

Foul bookings

In 1980, York City came up with an original design for their shirts – broad stripes from each shoulder which joined up and ran down the front to form the letter Y. What they hadn't thought about was the nickname they'd get – the Y-Fronts!

Football training

⚽⚽⚽⚽⚽⚽⚽⚽⚽⚽⚽⚽⚽⚽⚽⚽⚽⚽

....

Skills I'm best at

....

Skills I need to get better at

....

Record number of keepy uppys

....

Even the best footie players need lots of practice to keep playing well. Keep a record of the skills you are practising and improvements you have made over the next couple of pages...

Skills I am practising

....

....

....

....

....

....

....

....

....

Improvements I have made

....

....

....

....

....

....

....

....

....

In the early days of football, using a ball in training was thought to be a foul way of doing things. The players simply ran around and did exercises to keep fit. The idea behind this was that, by not seeing a football all week, when Saturday came around they'd want it all the time.

TEAM PROFILE

Quick quote

Life is great when your team is at the top of the League. But when you're down at the other end, football can really seem foul...

My team

⚽⚽⚽⚽⚽⚽⚽⚽⚽⚽⚽⚽⚽⚽⚽⚽⚽⚽

My football team
....

Team nickname
....

Home ground
....

How long I've supported my team
....

My fave players:
....

1.
....

2.
....

3.
....

Foulest player
....

Team manager
....

In 1988, replica kits went on sale in the shops for the first time. Now you could play for your favourite team in the park!

WE CAN'T PLAY AGAINST EACH OTHER, WE'RE IN DIFFERENT DIVISIONS!

Number of matches I went to last season:

Home

Away

Best match ever

Best goal ever

Team stuff I own

Team stuff I'd like to own

Team website address

Team info number

Ticket office number

For the whole of the 1992 season, Arsenal kicked towards a North Bank packed with fans who didn't move and didn't make a sound! The ground was being rebuilt, and the fans weren't real – they'd been painted on a massive board behind the goal.

Team prizes

◎◎◎◎◎◎◎◎◎◎◎◎◎◎◎◎◎◎◎◎

....

Cups won:

....

FA Cup

....

....

European Cup

....

....

UEFA Cup

....

....

League championships won:

....

....

....

....

Since the Villa side of the 1890s, no team pulled off the "Double" of winning both the League and the FA Cup in the same season until Tottenham managed it in 1960.

Team predictions

⚽⚽⚽⚽⚽⚽⚽⚽⚽⚽⚽⚽⚽⚽⚽⚽⚽⚽⚽⚽

What do you think is going to happen to your team this season?
Write down your predictions here, and check out if you're right in ten months' time...

....

What League position will they finish in?

....

What prizes will they win?

....

....

Who will be the top goal scorer?

....

Which players will leave?

....

....

....

Which players will join?

....

....

....

Between 1972 and 1991, Liverpool were either champions or runners-up in the League every year but one (the odd year out was 1980–81, when they finished fifth).

KICK-OFF

Quick quote

Robert Vidal, who played for Oxford University in 1873, was nicknamed "Prince of Dribblers". In those days the rule was that the team that scored also kicked off. Once, Vidal scored three goals in a match without the other team touching the ball!

Key dates

⚽⚽⚽⚽⚽⚽⚽⚽⚽⚽⚽⚽⚽⚽⚽⚽⚽⚽⚽⚽⚽

....

August

....

....

September

....

....

October

....

....

November

....

....

December

....

....

Back in 1882, when Spurs were formed (and simply called "Hotspur"), they had no ground or official meeting place – it's said that the players held meetings under a gas-light in Tottenham High Road.

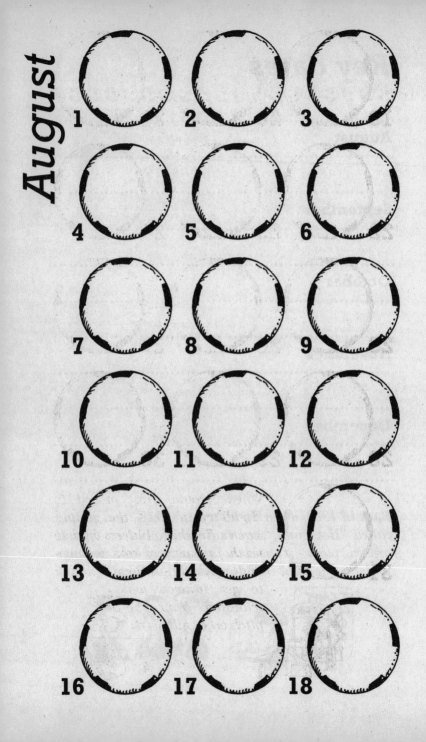

19 20 21

22 23 24

25 26 27

28 29 30

31

When Arsenal first moved to Highbury in 1913, the ground wasn't finished. Players had to wash in bowls of cold water – and anybody unlucky enough to get injured was trundled from the pitch on a milk cart.

GLUG! GLUG!

MILK

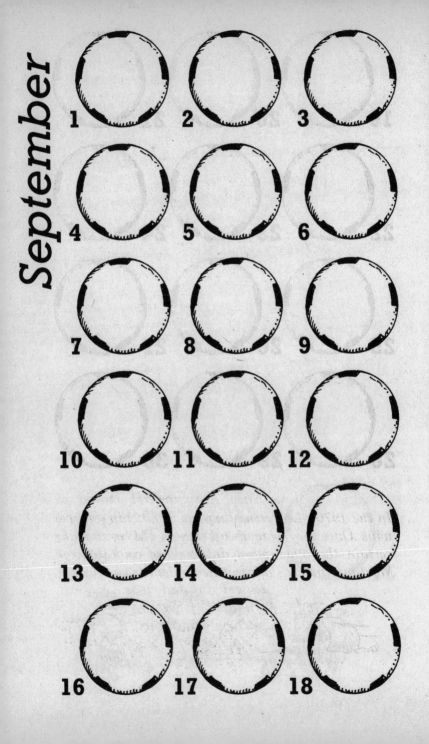

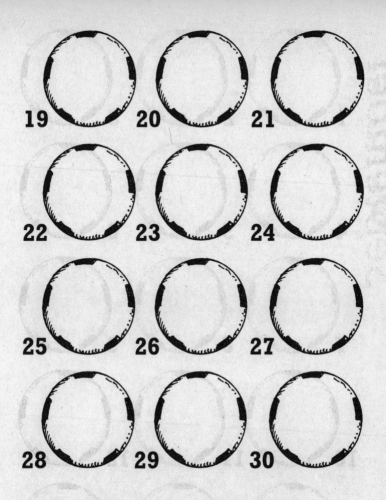

19   20   21

22   23   24

25   26   27

28   29   30

In the 1970s, Leeds were experts at notching up 1-0 wins. Once they were ahead they would try to make certain the other team didn't score an equalizer. Wasting time was a favourite tactic.

October

1 2 3
4 5 6
7 8 9
10 11 12
13 14 15
16 17 18

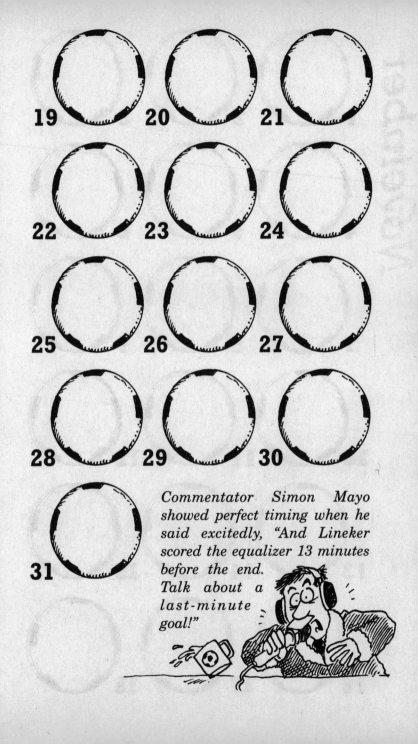

19 20 21

22 23 24

25 26 27

28 29 30

31

Commentator Simon Mayo showed perfect timing when he said excitedly, "And Lineker scored the equalizer 13 minutes before the end. Talk about a last-minute goal!"

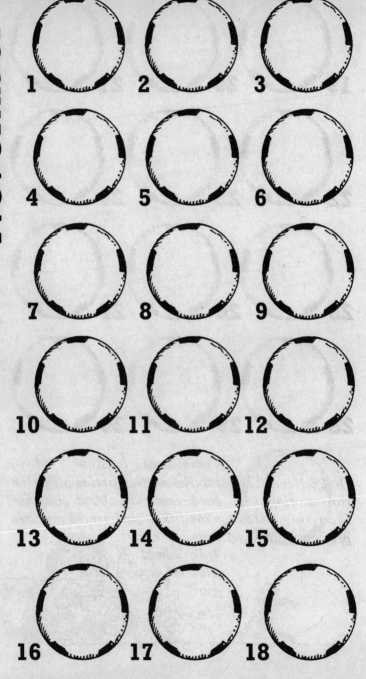

November

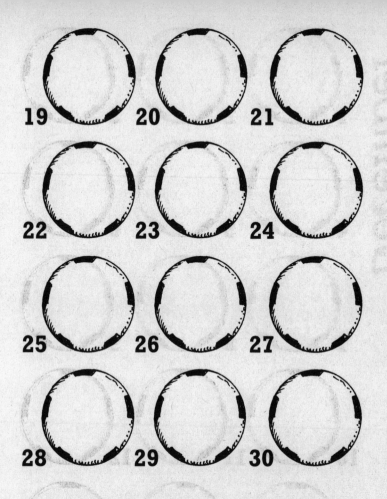

19 **20** **21**

22 **23** **24**

25 **26** **27**

28 **29** **30**

On 26 November 1983, Kenny Dalglish managed a rare scoring feat. He scored his 100th goal for Liverpool, matching the 100+ he'd scored for his previous club, Celtic.

December

1 2 3
4 5 6
7 8 9
10 11 12
13 14 15
16 17 18

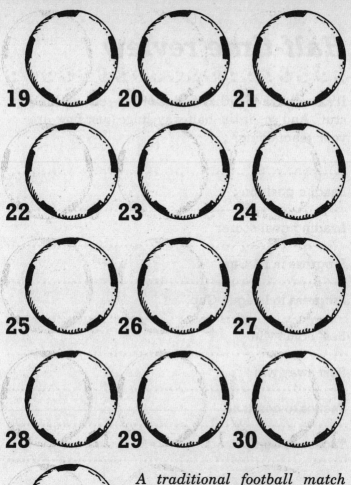

19 20 21

22 23 24

25 26 27

28 29 30

31

A traditional football match takes place every Christmas Day on Goodwin Sands, in Kent. Does one team manage to beach the other? Or are they always tide? Ha ha!

Half-time review

It's been five months of edge-of-the-seat nail-biting stuff. And so, at the half-way stage, just how are your team doing?

....

League position
....

Leading goal scorer
....

Progress in FA Cup
....

Progress in League Cup
....

Best home win
....

Best away win
....

Tactics to continue
....

Tactics to dump
....

When Terry Venables was manager of Crystal Palace in 1979, he called a hypnotist to work with the players. At the end of the season, Palace were promoted!

HALF-TIME TRIVIA

BETWEEN 1989 AND 1997 RANGERS EQUALLED CELTIC'S RECORD TO WIN THE SCOTTISH LEAGUE TITLE NINE TIMES IN A ROW...

Quick quote

Commentators often say some pretty daft things. Mick Lowes told his listeners, "And so it's West Ham 1, Everton 0, and that's the way it stayed through half-time…"

The ultimate fan's quick quiz

☺☺☺☺☺☺☺☺☺☺☺☺☺☺☺☺☺☺

Who's your favourite player? Is he a gallant goalkeeper or a super striker? A midfield maestro or a dangerous defender? Is he worth his weight in gold – or not even in pennies? Whatever you think of them, it's the players who make football the fantastic game it is – like the players in this quiz.

1 *Midget Gem* and *Blond Gerbil* have both been nicknames for – who?

a) Michael Owen.
b) David Beckham.
c) Rio Ferdinand.

2 When he signed for Newcastle United for a then-record £15 million, Alan Shearer was certainly pleased. He said, *I'm here for the rest of my life …* then added – what?
a) *And hopefully after that as well.*
b) *Unless I move somewhere else.*
c) *As long as I don't get injured.*

3 "Dixie" Dean of Everton was the Michael Owen of his day. In the 1927–28 season he scored a record 60 league goals, many of them with headers. Why was this surprising?
a) He wore glasses.
b) He'd once fractured his skull.
c) Heading made him dizzy.

4 In 1983, injury-hit Watford weren't in a position to pay a record fee but they were desperate for players. So they put an advertisement in *The Times* newspaper! What did it ask for?

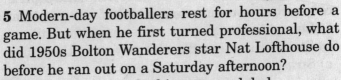

a) Male footballers.
b) Anybody with arms and legs.
c) Female footballers.

5 Modern-day footballers rest for hours before a game. But when he first turned professional, what did 1950s Bolton Wanderers star Nat Lofthouse do before he ran out on a Saturday afternoon?
a) All the shopping for his mum and dad.
b) Clean the boots of all the other Bolton players.
c) Finish his work at the bottom of a coal mine.

6 As we all know, football can be a foul game. What did Bayern Munich's player Giovane Elber say that Arsenal defender Tony Adams did to him when the two teams met in July 2000?
a) Pushed and kicked him.
b) Strangled his neck.
c) Pretended to shake his hand then stamped on his foot.

7 Ex-Wimbledon player Vinnie Jones was so proud of his foul play that he helped make a dirty fouls video. Not surprisingly he got into trouble for it.

Wimbledon chairman Sam Hamman explained away Jones's antics by saying he had – what?
a) A mosquito brain.
b) A bird brain.
c) A dinosaur brain.

8 Any goal is a good goal, but some are absolutely amazing. In 1952, Charlie Tully of Celtic scored a couple that were just that. How did he score them?
a) Straight from the kick-off.
b) Straight from a corner.
c) Straight from a goal-kick.

9 During a game in 1970, Bobby Moore of West Ham thumped the ball out of defence – and knocked out the referee! But what did he do next?
a) Blew the ref's whistle to stop the game.
b) Threw water over him.
c) Picked him up and carried him off the pitch.

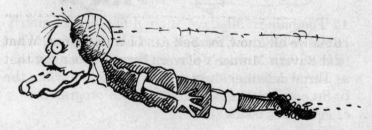

10 During the season we'll be cheering on our international players as they start their European Championship campaigns. Will there be some new faces – and, if so, will any of them do what Tottenham Hotspur's Bill Nicholson did in his first England game in 1951? Did he:

a) Get sent off with his first foul of the game.
b) Injure his goalkeeper with his first international tackle.
c) Score with his first touch of the ball.

11 We see daft goal celebrations all year round, but they're not a new invention. Hugo Sanchez, a Mexican international of the 1980s, used to celebrate every goal with a trick taught him by his sister. What was it?
a) A disco bum spin.
b) A curtsey.
c) A somersault.

THAT'S SOME GOAL CELEBRATION!

12 Footballers all have their different pre-match habits. What did Elisha Scott, a Liverpool favourite in the 1920s, always do for an hour before a game?
a) Throw a ball against a wall.
b) Sit on the loo and read the match programme.
c) Polish his boots.

13 The FA Cup gives players from tiny clubs a chance to get their names in the newspapers – like Billy Minter of St Albans City did in 1922 for scoring seven goals in their match against the equally little Dulwich Hamlet. But what else was remarkable about his feat?

a) Most of them were in his own net.
b) He still ended up on the losing side.
c) He started the game in goal.

14 There's big transfer money spent on players. But are they worth it? Even the players don't think so sometimes. When he was bought by Manchester United for £10.5 million pounds, what did Dutch International Jaap Stam say he'd seen built for less?
a) Shopping centres.
b) Hospitals.
c) Footballer's houses.

15 Finally, even as you're reading these words, somewhere in the world a future football star may be taking his first breath. Will his (or her) mum be able to tell? What did the doctors shout as Argentina's star Diego Maradona was born?
a) It's a goal!
b) It's a footballer!
c) It's a hand!

Answers:
1 a) *Blond Gerbil* at school and *Midget Gem* (after the sweets of the same name) at Liverpool.
2 a) Well, Newcastle fans say he plays like an angel!
3 b) In a motorbike accident.

4 a) OR c) The joke advert said the club was looking for men or women! But it insisted that they had two arms and legs *in working order*!

5 c) Then "dug out" his boots and went off to play!

6 All three! **a)** and **b)** during the match, and **c)** outside the dressing rooms after the game was over.

7 a) He couldn't think of anything smaller.

8 b) But only one counted. His first corner-goal was disallowed because fans were on the pitch so he took the corner again … and scored again!

9 a) Then somebody else threw water over him!

10 c) It was his only international goal, too. Nicholson was never picked for England again.

11 c) She was an Olympic gymnast.

12 a) He was Liverpool's goalkeeper and did it to practise his catching.

13 b) Amazingly, St Albans lost the game 8-7!

14 a) Then again, shopping centres aren't sold after two years; Stam was!

15 a) But only because they were football fans. Several girls had already been born that day and Maradona was the first boy to arrive.

HOW DID YOU SCORE?

12–15 Great stuff. Let's hope your favourite player scores equally well!

6–11 Decent performance. Your top man could have a patchy season.

0–5 Hmm. If your fave player performs like that he'll be up for sale!

SECOND HALF

THEY NEVER LET ME FINISH MY LUNCH

Quick quote

In 1955, Dennis Evans (Arsenal) heard a whistle and thought it was the ref blowing for the end of their match. So what did he do? He booted the ball into the net, only to discover that he'd scored an own goal! The whistle he'd heard had been blown by somebody in the crowd. Good job Arsenal were winning 4-0 at the time!

Key dates

⚽⚽⚽⚽⚽⚽⚽⚽⚽⚽⚽⚽⚽⚽⚽⚽⚽

....
January
....

....
February
....

....
March
....

....
April
....

....
May
....

....

It wasn't until 1969 that the FA finally recognized that women had a right to play football, too. Now there's a Women's FA, hundreds of women's football clubs, and a full programme of national and international competitions.

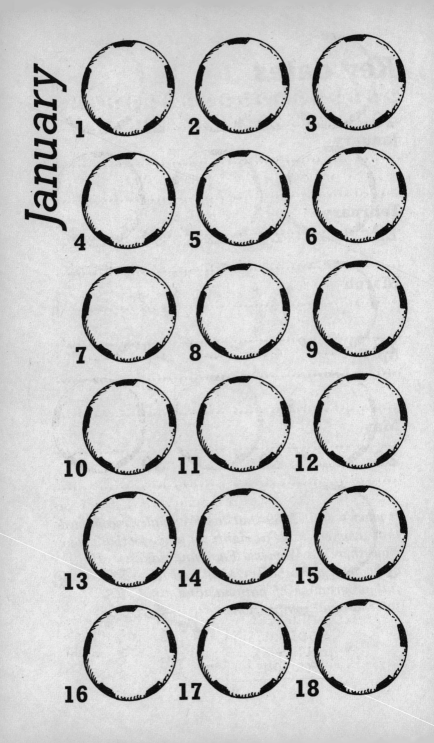

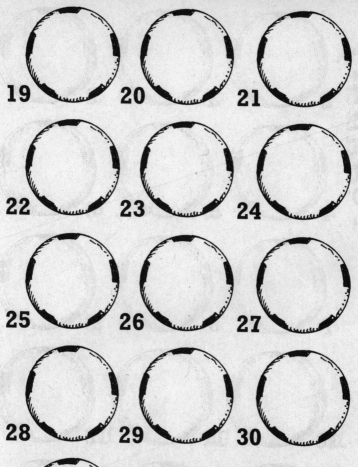

19   20   21

22   23   24

25   26   27

28   29   30

31

On 6 January 1934, Stockport County became the first team to win a League game 13-0. They were playing against Halifax Town in the Third Division (North) at the time.

THIRTEEN IS DEFINITELY UNLUCKY FOR SOME!

YES, YOU!

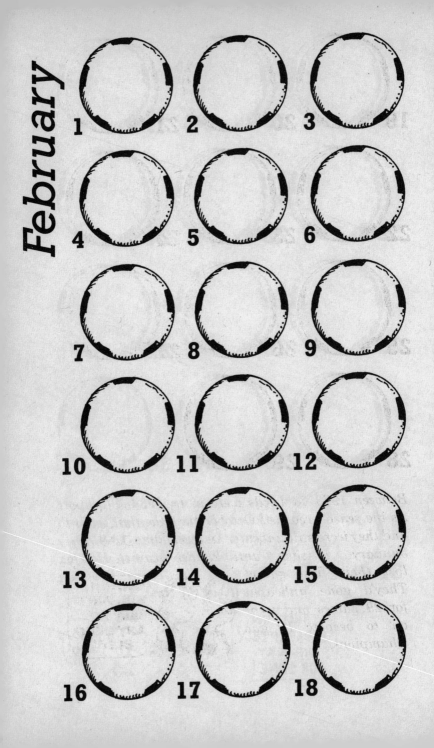

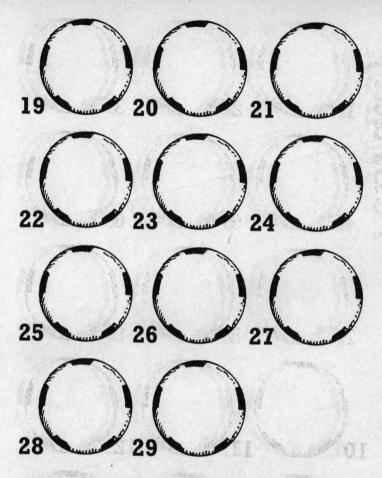

19 **20** **21**

22 **23** **24**

25 **26** **27**

28 **29**

Between 1973–74 Leeds were in tremendous form. As the season reached October they were unbeaten; and they were still unbeaten in November, December, January... It wasn't until 23 February that they lost their first game! They'd gone unbeaten for 29 games and went on to become League Champions.

WIN, WIN, WIN, DON'T THEY DO ANYTHING ELSE?

March

1 2 3
4 5 6
7 8 9
10 11 12
13 14 15
16 17 18

19 20 21

22 23 24

25 26 27

28 29 30

31

In 1996, a certain John Neilson, playing for Easthouses Lily in the East of Scotland League, was sent off. So what did Neilson do? Shout at the referee? Bop him on the nose? No. While the match was still going on, Neilson crept into the referee's changing room and cut his socks in half!

April

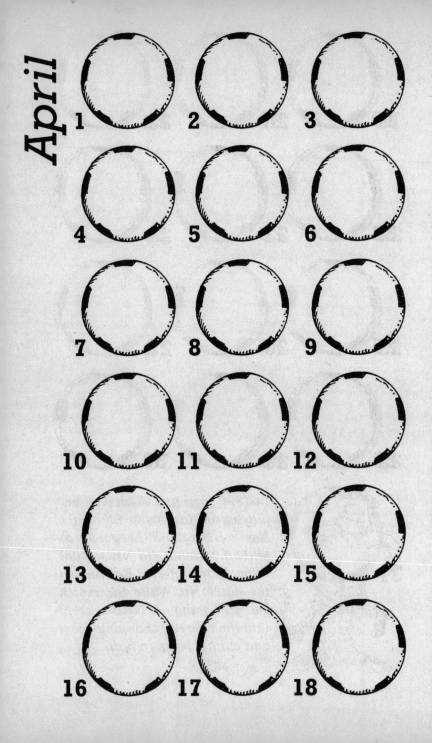

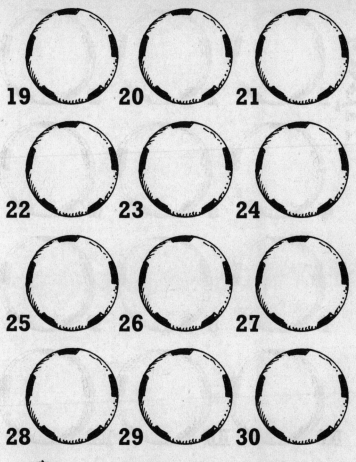

19 20 21

22 23 24

25 26 27

28 29 30

It was Scotsman William McGregor who came up with the brilliant idea of having a league competition for football teams, and on 17 April 1888, the formation of the Football League was announced.

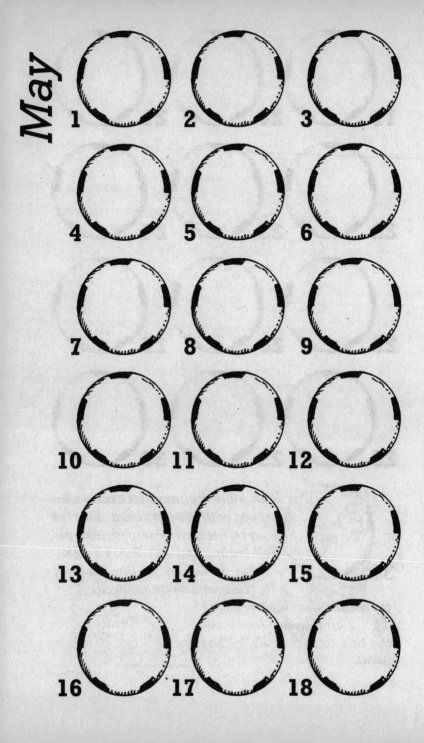

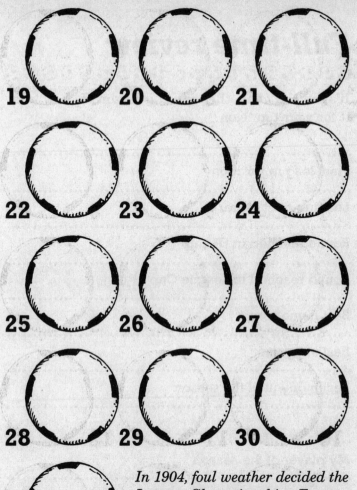

19 **20** **21**
22 **23** **24**
25 **26** **27**
28 **29** **30**
31

In 1904, foul weather decided the League Championship. Everton were beating Woolwich Arsenal 3-1 when fog came down and the game had to be abandoned. When the match was replayed, Everton lost 1-2 ... and ended the season losing the title to Newcastle by just one point.

Full-time review

⚽⚽⚽⚽⚽⚽⚽⚽⚽⚽⚽⚽⚽⚽⚽⚽⚽⚽

It's the end of another exciting season. So how was it for your top team?

....

Final league position

....

Leading goal scorer

....

Round reached in FA Cup

....

Round reached in League Cup

....

Best home win

....

Best away win

....

Best moment of the season

....

....

My player of the season

....

Between 1989 and 1997 Rangers equalled Celtic's record to win the Scottish League title nine times in a row.

EXTRA TIME

Quick quote

When penalties were invented in 1891, some FA members objected. They thought a penalty law suggested that some of their players were ungentlemanly ... which they were, of course!

Close season notes

✪✪✪✪✪✪✪✪✪✪✪✪✪✪✪✪✪✪✪✪✪✪✪

The season's finished, but it's not all over yet. There's plenty of footballing fun to be had in the close season and when the new season starts in August we've given you some extra time...

....

....

....

....

....

....

....

....

A favourite day for playing foot-balle (the medieval game of football) was Shrove Tuesday, the day we call "pancake day". Maybe this was because a lot of the players ended the game as flat as one.

I WISH SOMEONE WOULD INVENT A FOOTBALL!

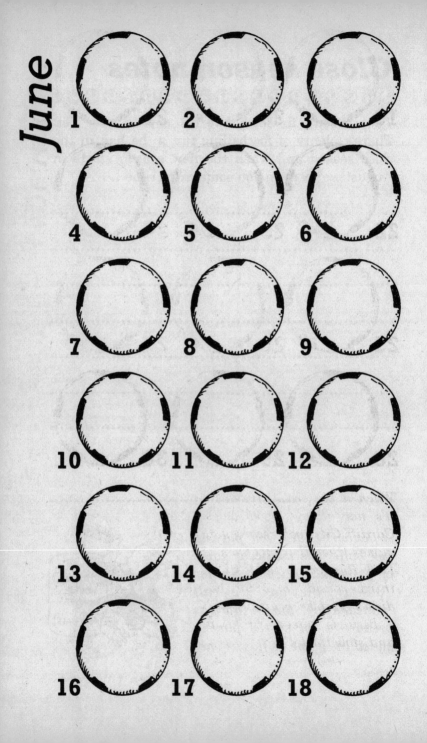

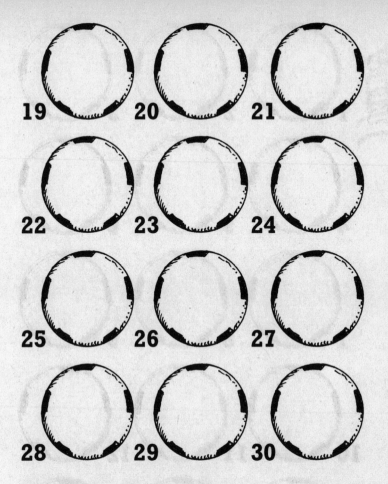

19 20 21

22 23 24

25 26 27

28 29 30

When a big crowd turns up it's not always good news. Cardiff City took record gate money when they met Queens Park Rangers in the FA Cup third round in 1990 but didn't get to keep a penny of it – because thieves broke in and stole the lot!

CHING! CHING!

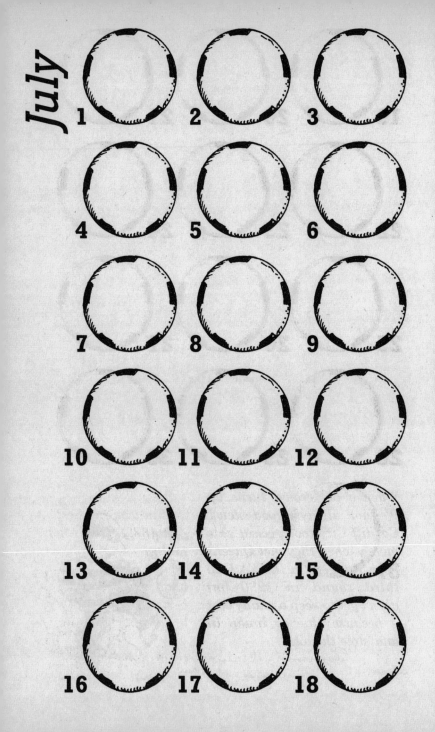

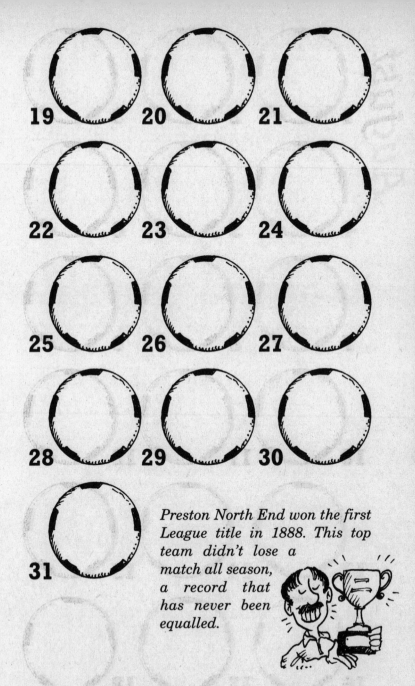

19
20
21
22
23
24
25
26
27
28
29
30
31

Preston North End won the first League title in 1888. This top team didn't lose a match all season, a record that has never been equalled.

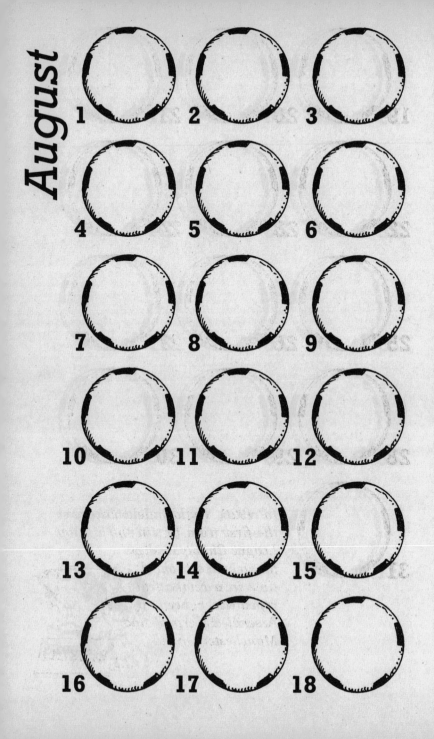

19   20   21

22   23   24

25   26   27

28   29   30

31

In 1926, Huddersfield became the first team to win the League Championship for a record third time in a row, a feat repeated only by Arsenal, Liverpool and Manchester United.

RESERVED!

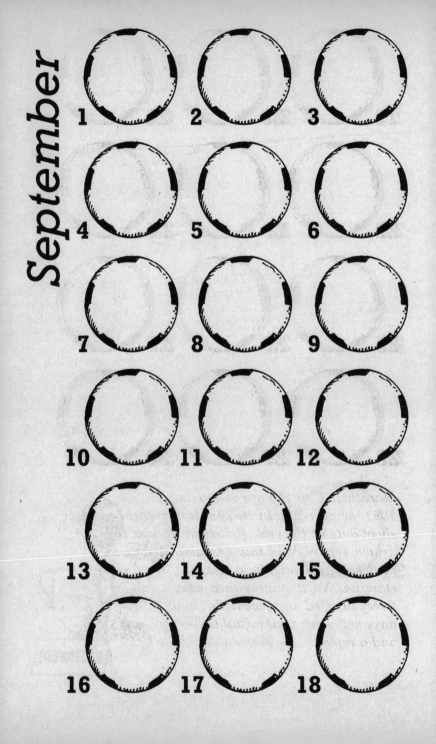

September

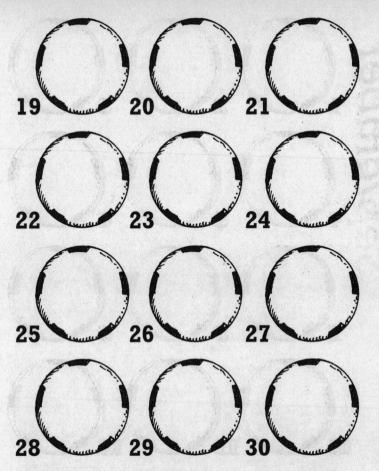

19 20 21

22 23 24

25 26 27

28 29 30

Marathon Cup replays ended in 1991, being replaced by penalty shoot-outs at the end of a single drawn replay. Was this because modern-day footballers lack the stamina? No, it was because police forces insisted on at least ten days notice between a Cup-tie and a replay.

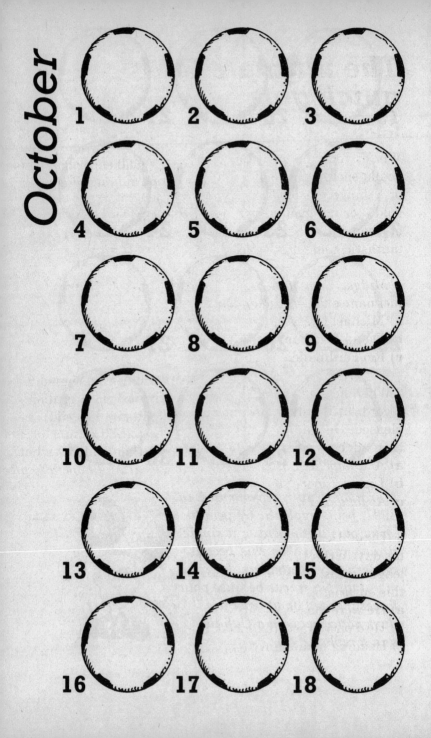

October

1 2 3
4 5 6
7 8 9
10 11 12
13 14 15
16 17 18

19 **20** **21** **22** **23** **24** **25** **26** **27** **28** **29** **30** **31**

In 1929, almost 50 years after playing their first international, England tasted defeat for the first time. They lost 4-3 to Spain. The newspapers blamed the heat, saying, "beads of perspiration were dropping off the chins of our players as they ran about"!

November

1 2 3
4 5 6
7 8 9
10 11 12
13 14 15
16 17 18

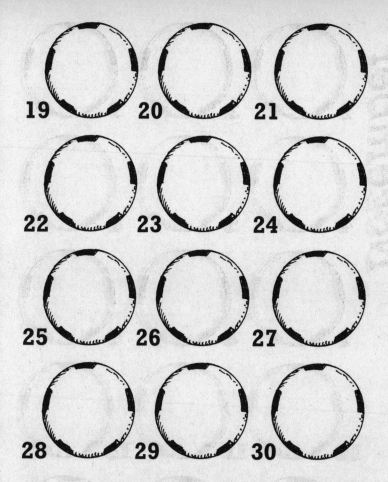

19 20 21

22 23 24

25 26 27

28 29 30

The first team ever to take the field for Liverpool only contained one Englishman, their goalkeeper. The other ten outfield players were all Scots.

December

1 2 3
4 5 6
7 8 9
10 11 12
13 14 15
16 17 18

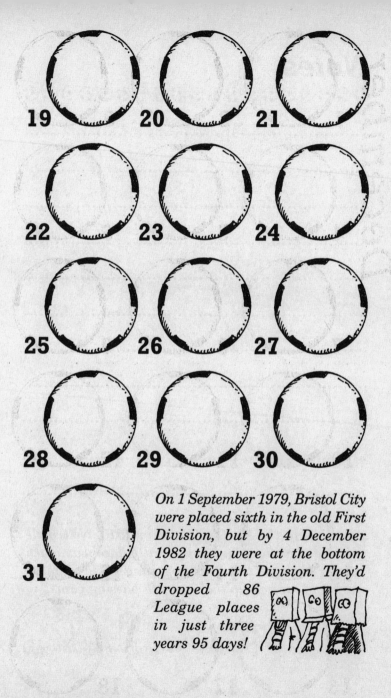

19 **20** **21**

22 **23** **24**

25 **26** **27**

28 **29** **30**

31

On 1 September 1979, Bristol City were placed sixth in the old First Division, but by 4 December 1982 they were at the bottom of the Fourth Division. They'd dropped 86 League places in just three years 95 days!

Notes

⚽⚽⚽⚽⚽⚽⚽⚽⚽⚽⚽⚽⚽⚽⚽⚽⚽⚽

....

....

....

....

....

....

....

....

....

....

After losing the FA Cup Final in 1910, Newcastle claimed that the grass at Crystal Palace was much thicker than at their home ground of St James's Park and messed up their smooth passing game!

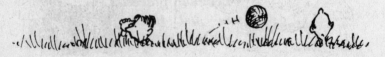

SEASON LOG

OOPS!

Quick quote

Only a top team can win the Football League Championship because only a top team is good enough to win matches throughout the sunny days of August, the wet days of November, the snowy days of January, the windy days of March until the season ends with some more sun in May.

Team League fixtures

Record your team's progress in the League over the next few pages.

Date	Opposition	Home/Away	Score	Scorers

Team League fixtures

Date	Opposition	Home/Away	Score	Scorers

Team League fixtures

Date	Opposition	Home/Away	Score	Scorers

FA Cup fixtures

Record your team's progress in the FA Cup over the next couple of pages.

Third Round

Date	Opposition	Home/Away	Score	Scorers
Replay				

Fourth Round

Date	Opposition	Home/Away	Score	Scorers
Replay				

Fifth Round

Date	Opposition	Home/Away	Score	Scorers
Replay				

FA Cup fixtures

Quarter Final

Date	Opposition	Home/Away	Score	Scorers
Replay				

Semi Final

Date	Opposition	Home/Away	Score	Scorers

Final

Date	Opposition	Home/Away	Score	Scorers

League Cup fixtures

Record your team's progress in the League Cup over the next couple of pages.

Second Round

Date	Opposition	Home/Away	Score	Scorers

Third Round

Date	Opposition	Home/Away	Score	Scorers

Fourth Round

Date	Opposition	Home/Away	Score	Scorers

Quarter Final

Date	Opposition	Home/Away	Score	Scorers

League Cup fixtures

Semi Final Home

Date	Opposition	Home/Away	Score	Scorers

Semi Final Away

Date	Opposition	Home/Away	Score	Scorers

Final

Date	Opposition	Home/Away	Score	Scorers

Cup fixtures

Record your team's progress in the other cup matches over the next few pages.

Cup	Date	Opposition	Home/Away	Score	Scorers
.....	.....	.....	.....	.....	.....
.....	.....	.....	.....	.....	.....
.....	.....	.....	.....	.....	.....
.....	.....	.....	.....	.....	.....
.....	.....	.....	.....	.....	.....
.....	.....	.....	.....	.....	.....
.....	.....	.....	.....	.....	.....
.....	.....	.....	.....	.....	.....
.....	.....	.....	.....	.....	.....
.....	.....	.....	.....	.....	.....
.....	.....	.....	.....	.....	.....
.....	.....	.....	.....	.....	.....

Cup fixtures

Cup	Date	Opposition	Home/Away	Score	Scorers

Cup fixtures

Cup	Date	Opposition	Home/Away	Score	Scorers

Transfers

⚽⚽⚽⚽⚽⚽⚽⚽⚽⚽⚽⚽⚽⚽⚽⚽⚽⚽

Every season sees old faces go and new faces
appear. Keep a record of the comings and goings of
your team's players on this page.

Name	Position	To/From	Fee

*Jimmy Greaves should have been the first £100,000
player when Spurs bought him from AC Milan. Bill
Nicholson, Spurs' manager, didn't want him to be
stuck with that honour though, so he got the Italians
to knock a pound off the fee!*

My views

⚽⚽⚽⚽⚽⚽⚽⚽⚽⚽⚽⚽⚽⚽⚽⚽⚽

What decisions would be made if *you* were managing your team? Now's your chance to have that say...

....

Best buy

....

Worst buy

....

Sad to see him go

....

Glad to see the back of

....

Which players we should sign

....

....

Which players we should drop

....

....

In 1919, Leeds City were expelled from the League. Their whole team was auctioned! Individual players fetched between £250 and £1,250, with the whole lot fetching a grand total of about £10,000! One of the £250 players was Bill Kirton. He was sold to Aston Villa – and scored the winning goal in the Cup Final!

Memorable matches

❂❂❂❂❂❂❂❂❂❂❂❂❂❂❂❂❂❂❂❂❂

What were the best matches your team played this season? Keep a record of the magic moments you have seen over the next couple of pages.

Date
....
Opponents
....
Home/Away
....
Score
....
Scorers
....
Man of the match
....
Bookings
....
Substitutions
....
Injuries
....
Memorable moments
....

....

❂❂❂

Date
....
Opponents
....
Home/Away
....
Score
....
Scorers
....
Man of the match
....
Bookings
....
Substitutions
....
Injuries
....
Memorable moments
....

....

Date
....
Opponents
....
Home/Away
....
Score
....
Scorers
....
Man of the match
....
Bookings
....
Substitutions
....
Injuries
....
Memorable moments
....

....

⚽ ⚽ ⚽

Date
....
Opponents
....
Home/Away
....
Score
....
Scorers
....
Man of the match
....
Bookings
....
Substitutions
....
Injuries
....
Memorable moments
....

....

*It's 1957 and Manchester United are playing Bolton
Wanderers in the FA Cup Final. With Bolton 1-0 up,
United's goalkeeper, Harry Gregg, saves a fierce shot
by pushing it up into the air. As it comes down
again, Bolton's Nat Lofthouse charges in and knocks
Gregg and the ball into the net for a goal!*

GAMES

Quick quote

The original FA Cup was bought for £20 and was 46 cm high. Its nickname was "the little tin idol".

Dream team

⚽⚽⚽⚽⚽⚽⚽⚽⚽⚽⚽⚽⚽⚽⚽⚽⚽⚽⚽⚽

Ever dreamed of being a football manager? Well now's your chance to create a terrific team of 11 prize players and see them perform throughout the season. Just like a real football team, choose players to a pattern something like:

one goalkeeper ⊙ **four** defenders ⊙ **three** forwards **three** midfield players ⊙ **three** substitutes

You then score points depending on how well the players perform in their team's games.

For goalkeepers and defenders you get:
3 points if their team doesn't let a goal in
-1 point for every goal their team does let in

For all players you get:
5 points for every goal they score
-10 points if they get sent off

You can choose to take a player off and bring on a substitute at any time throughout the season, but just as in a real game, once you've taken a player off the pitch, that's it until full time.

So put yourself in the manager hot-spot, choose a name for your team and their ground and start playing the dream team game. Get your mates to take part, too, then at the end of the season, tot up your points to find out who's done best.

Dream team

....

Manager

....

Dream team name

....

....

....

Football ground

....

....

Name

....

Position

....

Team

....

....

Name

....

Position

....

Team

....

Dream team

....

Name
....

Position
....

Team
....

....

Name
....

Position
....

Team
....

....

Name
....

Position
....

Team
....

....

Name
....

Position
....

Team
....

Dream team

....

Name

....

Position

....

Team

....

....

Name

....

Position

....

Team

....

....

Name

....

Position

....

Team

....

....

Name

....

Position

....

Team

....

Dream team

Name

....

Position

....

Team

....

Name

....

Position

....

Team

....

Name

....

Position

....

Team

....

Name

....

Position

....

Team

....

The Cheers and Boos Game

So you want to be a footballer. Try it by playing this game. The idea is to get more cheers than boos from the crowd.

THIS WAY →

KICK-OFF

FANTASTIC START TO YOUR CAREER

1 AT THE AGE OF 14, EAMONN COLLINS BECAME THE YOUNGEST LEAGUE PLAYER WHEN HE CAME ON AS SUB FOR BLACKPOOL.

I WOULD HAVE COME ON EARLIER BUT I HAD TO FINISH MY HOMEWORK FIRST!

SCORE THREE CHEERS!

HALF-TIME

GO ON TO NEXT PAGE...

10 GET IN THE ACTION STRAIGHT AWAY

ON 25 FEBRUARY 1984, COLIN HARRIS SCORED HIS 1ST GOAL WITH HIS 1ST TOUCH IN THE 1ST MINUTE. HE WAS ON THE FIELD IN HIS FIRST GAME FOR DUNDEE!

ZOOM!

SCORE O CHEERS

YOU WERE TOO QUICK FOR ANYONE TO SEE IT!

9

COME OUT OF THE RESERVES AND BANG IN TEN GOALS!

JOE PAYNE WAS A RESERVE WING-HALF WHEN HE WAS PICKED AS MAKE-SHIFT CENTRE FORWARD FOR LUTON'S GAME AGAINST BRISTOL ROVERS ON 13 APRIL 1936, SCORING TEN GOALS IN THEIR 12-0 WIN.

HUH! I'D HAVE SCORED AT LEAST 11.

8

SCORE 10 CHEERS

(AND 1 BOO FROM THE PLAYER REPLACED!)

SENT OFF FOR THE 1ST TIME

ENGLAND GOALKEEPER PETER SHILTON WAS SENT OFF FOR THE FIRST TIME WHEN PLAYING HIS 971ST GAME!

SCORE 970 CHEERS AND 1 BOO.

I HOPE YOU'RE NOT GOING TO MAKE A HABIT OF THIS, SHILTON.

13

14

SENT OFF, MURDERED AND BANNED.

15

IN 1995, LUIGI COLUCCIO, A CALABRIAN LEAGUE PLAYER IN ITALY WAS SENT OFF. A WEEK LATER HE WAS SHOT DEAD. EVEN SO, HE WAS STILL BANNED. WHY? BECAUSE IT COULD HAVE INFLUENCED THE END OF SEASON FAIR PLAY AWARDS.

SCORE 3 BOOS AND LEAVE THE GAME FOREVER!

THE GOOD NEWS IS THAT YOU CAN APPEAL AGAINST THE BAN NEXT SEASON

LUIGI COLUCCIO

DROPPED! HAROLD BELL PLAYED 459 CONSECUTIVE LEAGUE AND CUP GAMES FOR TRANMERE ROVERS BETWEEN 1946 AND 1955 BEFORE HE WAS DROPPED. **SCORE 1 BOO AND 3 CHEERS, MISS A GO, BUT COLLECT A LONG SERVICE AWARD**

MATCH PROG

BELL ISN'T PLAYING! I HOPE THE MANAGER HASN'T DROPPED A CLANGER!

17

16

97

The top-spot tournament

✪✪✪✪✪✪✪✪✪✪✪✪✪✪✪✪✪✪✪

This contest is just like a League competition. Why? Because it will last the whole season! Challenge your eagle-eyed mates and see which of you manages to score the most points.

Top-spot #1: Hairstyles
When David Beckham shaved all his hair off it came as a surprise to one of his sponsors, Brylcreem – because they make hair cream!
But shaven heads are still in fashion. How many can you spot in a single team during a match?

Team: ....
3 shaven heads	*20 points* ○
4 shaven heads	*30 points* ○
More than 4 shaven heads	*50 points* ○

Top-spot #2: Mazy dribbles
Ex-Preston player and Liverpool Manager Bill Shankley used to say about Preston's famous dribbling winger Tom Finney, *There'd be four men marking him – when we were kicking in!*

Players don't dribble with the ball so much nowadays. Top-spot those that do!

Player and team:...

3 players beaten	*20 points*	○
4 players beaten	*30 points*	○
More than 4 players beaten	*50 points*	○

Top-spot #3: Aaargh, it's me leg!
Injuries are part of the game, although not many players get hurt in such a daft way as Everton and ex-England star Paul Gascoigne – he once pulled a muscle getting out of bed! Not all injuries are as serious as they look. Top-spot one that isn't.

Player and team:...
Player comes back less than 5 mins after being carried off   *20 points* ○
Player comes back less than 2 mins after being carried off   *40 points* ○
Player who jumps off the stretcher   *100 points* ○

Top-spot #4: Player interviews
Footballers don't always talk a lot of sense straight after a game. In his Arsenal days Paul Merson, asked what he liked most about manager Arsene Wenger, said *He gives you unbelievable belief in yourself!*

Whoever the player, you can expect them to slip a few *y'knows* into the interview. Top-spot (or, rather, top-hear) them:

Player:...

1 or 2 y'knows	*10 points* ○
3, 4, or 5 y'knows	*30 points* ○
6, 7 or 8 y'knows	*50 points* ○
More than 8 y'knows	*100 points* ○

Top-spot #5: Squad numbers

The first football shirt owned by Bobby Charlton, Manchester United star of the 1960s and 70s, wasn't a replica bought from a shop – it was made by his mum out of an old pair of curtains!

Shirts nowadays have squad numbers on the back. Top-spot the largest number you can.

YOUR MUM'S STILL MAKING YOUR KIT, THEN?

Player and team:..

Squad number over 20	*10 points* ○
Squad number over 30	*20 points* ○
Squad number over 40	*50 points* ○
Squad number over 99	*100 points* ○

Top-spot #6: Super substitutes
In the 1999 European Champions League Final, Manchester United beat Bayern Munich 2-1 with two goals being scored in the last two minutes. What's more the goalscorers, Teddy Sheringham and Ole Gunnar Solksjaer, weren't on the pitch at the start of the match – they were super-subs, coming on late in the game. Top-spot the latest-scoring substitute in the games you watch.

Substitute and team: ....

Sub scoring before the 80th minute	*20 points* ○
Sub scoring between the 80th and 90th minutes	*30 points* ○
Sub scoring in time added on	*50 points* ○

Top-spot #7: Stupid celebrations
If Bobby Moore, England's World-Cup-winning captain, ever scored a goal for his club side, West Ham, he would celebrate in a very odd way – he'd just run back to the centre-circle for the kick-off. Nowadays that would never do. Top-spot some of the madder goal celebrations.

Shirt pulled over head	10 points ◯
Shirt over head and slogan T-shirt underneath	
	20 points ◯
Run and slide on the ground	25 points ◯
Wiggle at corner-flag	30 points ◯
Kiss a team mate's bald head	50 points ◯
Kiss the referee and get sent off	250 points ◯

Top-spot #8: Players enjoying themselves
During one game between Leeds and Leicester City in the 1960s, Leeds defender Jack Charlton ambled up for a corner to find Leicester's goalkeeper Gordon Banks pointing to where he wanted his defenders to go. What did Charlton do? Grabbed Banks's finger between his teeth and refused to let go! The joke made the other players laugh – a sight rarely seen nowadays it seems. So, for the hardest top-spot of all...

Team: ....

2 different players smiling or laughing	◯
20 points	
3 or 4 different players smiling or laughing	◯
30 points	
Any player having a joke with the referee	◯
50 points	

GRAND TOTAL OF POINTS AT THE END OF THE SEASON ....

HOW DID YOU GET ON?
Over 450 points: Wow! You must have eyes like a hawk. Ever thought of being a referee?
200–449 points: Pretty good. Your eyes don't need testing.
Under 200 points: Not so good. Are you a referee, by any chance?

The dreams and nightmares game

☺ ☺ ☺ ☺ ☺ ☺ ☺ ☺ ☺ ☺ ☺ ☺ ☺ ☺ ☺ ☺ ☺ ☺ ☺

Foul fans will watch plenty of games throughout the coming season. They'll hope that their team will always play like a dream – but they know that sometimes they'll have a nightmare!

Here's a game to get you prepared. Find a fellow foul fan and both try answering these questions. Take it in turn to choose your answer first, with the other player having to take the answer that's left. The fan who gets the right answer scores a goal and the one with the most goals wins. Will your game turn out to be a dream – or a nightmare?

1 Trevor Francis had just become the first £1 million player when he ran on to the pitch for his debut game with Nottingham Forest. **Dream or nightmare?**

2 Bill "Fatty" Foulke was a huge goalkeeper weighing 20 stone (127 kgs). In 1897 he was picked for his only international for England against Wales. **Dream or nightmare?**

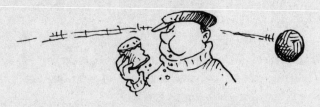

3 Tony Coton had been in goal for just 80 seconds in his debut game for Birmingham City against Sunderland when he got his first touch of the ball in league football. **Dream or nightmare?**

4 Manchester United legend Denis Law scored with a cheeky back-heel in a vital end-of-season game at Old Trafford in 1974. Did Law think the goal was a **Dream or nightmare?**

5 In 1953 England had a nightmare game against Hungary, losing their first-ever match at Wembley against an overseas team 6-3. The following year they travelled to Hungary in search of revenge. **Dream or nightmare?**

6 Giancarlo Antognoni helped Italy beat Poland in the 1982 World Cup semi-finals. In the final Italy met Germany. **Dream or nightmare?**

7 The first-ever match at Wembley was the 1923 FA Cup Final. Did it turn out to be a **Dream or nightmare?**

8 After three minutes of their 1965 FA Cup Final against Leeds, Liverpool's Gerry Byrne breaks his collar bone. **Dream or nightmare?**

9 Frank Swift played in goal for Manchester City against Portsmouth in the 1934 FA Cup Final when he was only 19 years old. Did he have a **Dream or nightmare?**

Answers:

1 Nightmare – Manager Brian Clough had sent Francis out to play for the 3rd team, in front of 20 fans.

2 Dream – Foulke kept a clean sheet as England won 4-0.

3 Dream – Coton had saved a penalty.

4 Nightmare – Because he'd been transferred to rivals Manchester City and was playing for them. His goal won City the game 1-0 and United were relegated.

5 Nightmare – An even bigger one; this time England lost 7-1.

6 Nightmare – Italy won, but Antognoni had been injured in the semi-final and couldn't play.

7 Nightmare – Such a big crowd turned up that they spilled on to the pitch. The match was only played at all because mounted policeman managed to push the fans back to the touchline.

8 Dream – Byrne played on, including extra-time, and Liverpool won 2-1.

9 Dream – Manchester City won ... and Swift fainted! (Whether he had a dream or a nightmare while he was unconscious isn't known.)

The ultimate fan's guide to football-speak

⚽⚽⚽⚽⚽⚽⚽⚽⚽⚽⚽⚽⚽⚽⚽⚽⚽⚽

When you watch a game on TV or listen to it on the radio there's always a commentator telling you what's going on. Even when play stops the talking carries on, with half-time experts and full-time interviews. What do you need to understand it all? This guide to football-speak, of course! Check out these top terms, then try giving your own match commentary!

Football-speak	What does it mean?	But ... what could it mean?
Action replay	TV shows an exciting incident again	TV shows an incident again hoping it'll be more exciting in slow motion
Avoid the drop	Avoid relegation	Avoid being hanged for missing a penalty
Caught in possession	Losing the ball	Being found sneaking home with the gate money
Dive	Forward falls over pretending to be fouled	Action defender makes to referee after he's fouled the forward
Goalkeeper	Player allowed to hold the ball in his hands	Player who holds his head in his hands when he doesn't hold the ball in his hands

Football-speak	What does it mean?	But ... what could it mean?
"Here we go..."	Happy refrain sung by fans when their team are winning	Miserable words muttered by fans streaming away from the ground with their team losing 5-0
Hit the woodwork	Hit the goal post with a shot	Hit referee on the head with a shot
Man of the match	Best player in the game	Player who can't give up smoking even though he knows it's bad for him
Manager	Man who picks the team	Man who goes mental because the team he picked is getting smashed
Overlap	Player runs outside another to receive a pass	Player does a silly thing with his shirt after scoring
Over the moon	Phrase used by happy player to say how he's feeling	Player tries to do an unbelievably silly thing with his shirt after scoring
Penalty area	Section of the pitch where the defending team can't form a wall for a free kick	Area of the body players protect with their hands when they are allowed to form a wall for a free kick

Football-speak	What does it mean?	But ... what could it mean?
Players tunnel	The place where players shake hands before a game	The place where players fight after a game
Referee	Man responsible for making sure the players stick to the rules	Man insulted by players who don't know the rules of the game they're supposed to be playing
Striker	Player who's in the team to score goals	Player who's refused to play any more because he thinks the team doesn't score enough goals
Super-sub	Player who's sent on by his manager and ends up scoring the winning goal	Player the manager didn't think was good enough to get in the team to begin with
Yellow card, red card	Shown by the referee to naughty players	Cards which often lead to players making naughty signs at the referee

My match commentary

⚽⚽⚽⚽⚽⚽⚽⚽⚽⚽⚽⚽⚽⚽⚽⚽⚽

Pre-match build-up

....

....

....

....

....

First half

....

....

....

....

....

....

My match commentary

....
....
....
....
....
....

Half-time analysis

....
....
....
....
....
....

My match commentary

Second half

....

....

....

....

....

....

....

....

....

....

....

My match commentary

Post-match player interview

....

....

....

....

....

Round-up

....

....

....

....

....

....

ADDRESSES

Quick quote

Yes, the headmaster of Donington Grammar School in Lincolnshire really did enter his team in the first-ever FA Cup competition in 1872. He thought his boys needed good healthy exercise and this was one of his enterprising schemes for giving it to them.

My mates
⚽⚽⚽⚽⚽⚽⚽⚽⚽⚽⚽⚽⚽⚽⚽⚽

....

Name

....

Address

....

....

Telephone

....

Email

....

Fave football team

....

....

Name

....

Address

....

....

Telephone

....

Email

....

Fave football team

....

HOW DID YOUR TEAM GET ON TODAY?

WE WOULD HAVE WON, IF WE'D SCORED MORE GOALS!

117

My mates

⚽⚽⚽⚽⚽⚽⚽⚽⚽⚽⚽⚽⚽⚽⚽⚽⚽⚽

....

Name

....

Address

....

....

Telephone

....

Email

....

Fave football team

....

....

Name

....

Address

....

....

Telephone

....

Email

....

Fave football team

....

WHAT SHOULD I USE TO CLEAN MY BOOTS?

My mates

⚽⚽⚽⚽⚽⚽⚽⚽⚽⚽⚽⚽⚽⚽⚽⚽⚽

Name
....

Address
....

....

Telephone
....

Email
....

Fave football team
....

....

Name
....

Address
....

....

Telephone
....

Email
....

Fave football team
....

YOUR
YOUNGER
BROTHER

My mates

⚽⚽⚽⚽⚽⚽⚽⚽⚽⚽⚽⚽⚽⚽⚽⚽

....
Name
....
Address
....

....
Telephone
....
Email
....
Fave football team
....

....
Name
....
Address
....

....
Telephone
....
Email
....
Fave football team
....

HOW WET WAS THE PITCH TODAY?

My mates

⚽⚽⚽⚽⚽⚽⚽⚽⚽⚽⚽⚽⚽⚽⚽⚽⚽⚽

....

Name

....

Address

....

....

Telephone

....

Email

....

Fave football team

....

....

Name

....

Address

....

....

Telephone

....

Email

....

Fave football team

....

OUR
TEAM
PLAYED
IN
FLIPPERS

121

Useful addresses

⚽⚽⚽⚽⚽⚽⚽⚽⚽⚽⚽⚽⚽⚽⚽⚽⚽⚽⚽⚽

The Football Association
25 Soho Square
London
W1D 4FA
www.the-fa.org

· ·

The Scottish Football Association
Hampden Park
Glasgow
G42 9UY
www.scottishfa.co.uk

· ·

Fédération Internationale de Football Association
FIFA House
P.O. Box 85
8030 Zürich,
Switzerland
www.fifa.com

· ·

The World Cup Archive
www.worldcuparchive.com

· ·

World Soccer Magazine
www.countrylife.co.uk/worldsoccer/index.htm

AUTOGRAPHS

Quick quote

In the 1939 FA Cup Final, Portsmouth played hot favourites Wolverhampton Wanderers. They were so famous that the Portsmouth team asked them for their autographs!

Autographs

Autographs

Autographs

Foul Football
From the first mad matches with a pig's bladder to the cracking competions of the 21st Century, this glorious guide will give you the score.

Wicked World Cup
This international guide gives you the coolest commentary on the biggest, best, most talked-about tournament there is.

Phenomenal F.A. Cup
Following the highs and lows of this awesome tournament, meet the giants and giant killers on the hazardous road to Wembley.

Triumphant Teams
From winning Wanderers to majestic Man U, this guide features the star squads from every decade of English football history.

Legendary Leagues
Discover top facts about legendary champions of the English and Scottish leagues from the early beginnings to the present day.

Furious Euro's
This goal-scoring guide tackles the pain and glory of the European Championships.

If you want to be in the game, get Foul Football!